Forward Pr...

...erry '97 A Winter's Ta...
...g on the Air... Solstic...
...s Sick Scents Baptism Bastard Change Arm...
...liseum Winter Music-Maker Reality Repris...
...nderstood Dysfunctional... Flight Path o...
...l the Fells The Generation Gap Woman Black...
...arden Before Rain Sophie Fighting Back Hom...
...ms She Sleeps in My Heart Pagan Dance ...
...ra in Winter A Dark Paradise Washing U...
...ember, One Summer Aurelia's Hands Butterflie...
...The Love That Dare Not speak its Name Drowne...
...ntinuity Cast a Dark Shadow Isle of Ewe ...
...Children's Cemetery Montserrat Caballé In...
...The Soulless Lair The Beast of Zion Lawrenc...
...he Water Tower Quietude Kismet The Victim...
...d Last Drop The First ... Gir...
...Beside Still Waters ... ack...
...Desire In Flanders F... ...rte...
...e The Apple Tree Co... ...we...
...eaps Smoke on the M... ...ing...
...isit Fingernails B... of...
...rst Time The Chase The Unborn Child Ove...
...ster Neglect The Sands of Changi Beach...

TOP 100
POETS
2002

Edited by Ian Walton

First published in Great Britain in 2002 by
POETRY NOW - An imprint of Forward Press Ltd.
Remus House,
Peterborough, PE2 9JX
Telephone (01733) 898101
Fax (01733) 313524

ISBN 0-75432-856-2

FOREWORD

For the fourth year running Forward Press is pleased and proud to announce the results of the Top 100 Poets Award.

For the first two years Ian Walton, founder and Chairman of Forward Press Ltd, himself a published poet, was the sole arbiter of the poems. Last year, in the belief that this would provide a balanced approach to the selection, the decisions were taken by a team of imprint managers, headed by Ian. This year, the team was extended from three to four, including Ian, and I was invited to add the final full stop.

James Feeke, Natalie Nightingale, Katie Coles and Kelly Oliver (all editors of respective imprints) Ian and myself brought over 200 years of experience to this process. All very different people, each with differing tastes, brought a valuable, if time-consuming, dimension to the final conclusion.

Throughout the course of the year, and from over fifty thousand entries, the editorial teams select and put forward those poems that in some way 'impact' on them. It was this huge collection of poems that were presented to the selection panel. All poems were read blind; no names, no addresses etc on the copies and a short list of about one thousand were agreed on by a points system. The process then began again. Eventually a hundred were chosen and the really serious debate and discussion began at this point. It was no easy task to reduce a list of this quality to the final seventeen who would collect more than fifty pounds and then to pick the major prize winners.

Any one of the poems in this book could have claimed the three thousand pounds. *Our Mother Was An Amazon* by Jane Seabourne brought a wry smile, Ian Clark's *Sick Scents* a warning and who has not felt the weight of 'clod-clung' boots in C Williamson's *Stone Age*?

And so evolved the final three: *Eustacia's Heath; Elderberry '97; A Winter's Tale*.

Pauline Kirk's *Elderberry '97* which evocatively illuminates the invisible thread between two women across two generations so nearly won the day. As did R N Taber's vivid description of sunset in *A Winter's Tale*. However, there can only be one winner and this year's unanimous vote was cast in favour of Lorna Meehan's *Eustacia's Heath*. The impact of this poem is unquestionable: the tribute to Thomas Hardy's work indisputable and, we feel, worthy of a reciprocal tribute were he still alive. The power of each line will leave the reader breathless.

Thank you to all the poets who sent their work to Forward Press during 2001, particularly those whose work I have had the honour of reading during this process of selection.

Poetry is, above all, an approach to the truth of feeling . . .

(Muriel Rukeyser)

Ann Johnson-Allen

CONTENTS & PRIZE WINNERS LIST

£3,000 Prize

£500 Prizes

£250 Prizes

£100 Prizes

£50 Prizes

£50 Prizes continued...

£50 Prizes continued...

Eustacia's Heath

(Her presence brought memories of Bourbon roses, rubies tropical midnights - Thomas Hardy - 'The Return of the Native')

And you sit and watch your sand run out,
With fragile dreams of faded grandeur.

With your hair like ebony evenings,
Your eyes blindly searching far and wide.
Your hollow rooms sigh with your solitude
And their dark corners offer no place to hide.

Gluttonous freedom,
Starved suffering.
A prison without bars
And secrets,
Too many secrets
And so little time.

It's not your fault the lovers love without love,
That you had a map to infinity and never found it.
It's not the fantastic flame's fault,
If the maddened moths must dance around it.

And you're desperate to remember the scent
Of your shattered glass roses.
They whisper cruelly with wonder,
And say nothing at all.
He built you a pedestal to a soft, safe heaven,
Do you expect him to catch you when you finally fall?

You will fall through his insecure promises, lost goddess,
And the fat black night and its blood will choke you.
And what an irony that you asked it to come,
And stain all the good you've ever done!
And what a tragedy that it could never tame you,
Wild lover!

Your silent serenity scratches his thin soul,
He sees his future and it hasn't happened yet,
And though your compassion lets him forgive,
Your passion will never let him forget,
And never have you looked more beautiful
Burning fire child,
As you do now in docile death.

Lorna Meehan

Elderberry '97

Writing out the label, I pause,
recalling a narrow track and berries in '97.
A witch of old in my kitchen,
I siphon summers into demijohns.
That July was good for strawberries,
this a sour one, needing extra sugar.

Suddenly, in a saucepan lid,
I see my grandmother's face,
distorted above a flowered pinnie.
'Try my dandelion,' she insists,
and salving her Methodist guilt,
adds, 'It's home-made - not alcoholic.'

Not alcoholic!
A glass of Granny's dandelion
would unfreeze a politician's hand.
Her elderflower made our Christmas carols
twice as jolly. Gran's arts were needed, too,
with a gale off the lane and under her door.

Sometimes, though, her magic was too strong.
On hot nights, corks would pop in the scullery,
setting us laughing in fright, while wine ran
like revolutionary hordes towards us.
I wonder how Gran would judge me now?
She would scorn my new-fangled gadgets,

having never fathomed a vacuum cleaner;
consider my central heating soft
and my education beyond my station.
Still, I think she would smile
and pass me a glass of her elderberry,
one witch to another.

Pauline Kirk

A Winter's Tale

A massive spearhead of shadow
invades the glorious sunset
(once victorious sunset!)
pierces each violet vein of light
till bloody streamers
blot the moon

Weasel lurks at the edge of moody ice,
a phantom of this half-world

Watch the sun dying,
my dying Son;
See the spidery moonlight spread
like tardy concerns on Judgement Day
as ghosts of our recent dead
come out to play.

R N Taber

Stone Age

There is something about him,
This man standing
At the open gate
Of an empty field.

He stands in his element;
Four-square,
Broad bottomed,
Fists thrust into pockets.
Rooted
To this spot.
Planted.
Heeled in by clod-clung ancestral boots,
Dug hard into the soil.

In a landscape of loam and fine tilth
He is clay:
Becoming flint.

It's a slow process,
This bone becoming stone.
It goes a knuckle at a time,
Growing
Substance out of fortitude,
Matter out of resolve;
Compacting iron-hard endurance
Out of equanimity.

He grows as a stone grows:
Locked in a fist of earth.
Enduring.

C Williamson

Our Mother Was An Amazon

When we were young,
our mother's knack of swooping
at the exact moment
of our wrongdoing
was so uncanny:
so sudden and terrible,
we called her
'Attila the Mum'

But if you had seen in those last years
you might have taken her for
a Little Old Lady:
silver-haired,
Dannimacked,
Hush-Puppied
with a penchant for
the Queen Mother.

Inclined to say 'oof'
when she rose from a chair
and get the giggles when
we tried to prise her into low-slung cars.

She held court in the hairdresser's
where, with bold malapropism and
a broad-brush feel for detail,
she would pronounce on village affairs.

That was another assumed identity.

The truth is that, by then,
she had become -
post-operatively -
an Amazon.

Jane Seabourne

Hanging On The Air . . .

She sits there, restless eyes, fingers twirling strand of hair,
Trying to hide her pain, but it hangs on the air
Between us.
Tenacious yet elusive, its face evades us,
Neither of us prepared to reach out and catch it,
Or look at it, or touch it;
Afraid perhaps of its sting,
Its backlash, its ugliness.
And I sit there with restless love -
Longing to slip past her pain
And hug her.
But they come as a pair, the two of them together;
And I cannot bear to touch pain's roughness again so soon.
Too fragile, me, for now.

Suffering in silence thus, the two of us sit -
Empathy and anguish hanging on the air -
Each waiting for the other to make a move.
And her pain knows me too well.
It will have me sooner or later.
And she sits there reaching out,
Restless eyes, fingers twirling strand of hair -
Waiting.

Jenny Proom

Solstice

When jagged ice speared the heart
And the sun,
A red ball, far off,
Gave light, but no heat,
Our progenitors waited,
Stood silent in snow,
Waited for the last red dawn
Before night coffined all.

Then he paused
The sun paused,
Drawn back like a chariot of fire,
Red sun in a world of white frost.

We have grown so wise
That only children believe
In the red and white man from the north -
The priest who called back the sun.
So wise we can gash the sky
And let darkness in.

What gift will the children receive?
Will they see the last dawn?

Ruth Albert

Violets

she has stopped dusting the figurine
on the new mantelpiece.
spits into its face
a blueish-white face
delicately ugly but perfectly innocent.

memories intrude at random
as she strokes the hard pleats
of the sculptured ballgown.
memories of her shy, hand-embroidered dress
covered in violets
long, without shoulder straps
pretending to be adult
extravagantly modest
fragrantly light and vulnerable.

the figurine has slipped from her hand.

she brushes the blue and white heap of
pain under the carpet.

Alfa

The Wagtail

Amid the rush of crystal streams
Where sunlight shafts on mossy banks
Where catkins drip with river dew
And misty gloom hangs low and dank
The wagtail skips from shore to rock
And back.

A creature void of vanity
But gifted with a wondrous style
No audience beholds his tricks
Yet he performs from dawn to dusk
And even then his tail still wags
Awhile.

Is he yellow, grey, or pied?
The darkness masks his true array
Must the dusk his colour hide,
Rid the stream of one so gay
Rob it of his fine display.

And even now his dance goes on
Undaunted by the closing day
His silhouette the bank adorns
And shadows flit as he performs
His only guide the twilight grey.

A darting ghost he now becomes
His actions merge with misty shapes
The shadow flits away.

Christopher J Whelan

Of Golden Rings

Is this too late an age to sing a song,
While murmuring waters make their way along,
Of meadows on a summer's afternoon,
Which wait for night with its translucent moon
To tune the harmony of starlit choirs
For roses twin without their thorny briars?

Is this too late an age to conjure up
A woman's laughing face without the cup
Of bitter taste from apples red which said
When bled - this heart does surely yield to head?
Or yet is it still possible to know
A woman such and still delight to grow?

Is this too late an age for freedom's thrall
Upon the wild wind's sighing flying call
Winging a way through meadows green to say
The warrior who yearns the rose in May,
A maid beneath the moon will meet once more,
Who, many ages past, was his before?

Desmond Tarrant

Afterwards

I am home now
and the visions creep around my doorstep.

How came I home?
By trolley bus, soft into Dartford streets.

Her sixteen years are small
and, as the newest roses, crimson.

So must I their perfume squander
in the garden of my hours?

The door inexorably is slammed
and I would sleep but do not dare.

George Pearson

Sick Scents

The cold rain soaks my skin,
Feeling every ice-cold drop.
Corporate junk carpets the ground
Free advertising from the bin.
Waiting to be found.

Neon flames burn through my eyes
Blinding me to all I know,
Zombies torment on every street
Gathering behind an old disguise.
The salesman's great feat.

Faceless people huddled close,
Hearing only their lowly peers
Under the ghostly gaze of fate.
And who honestly knows,
What drives their hate?

The eyes of a coffee junkie
Taste a plagiarised life,
A hybrid of the ancient and perverse.
Caged like a lab monkey,
An eternity cursed.

Everything moulds into one,
Smells nauseous to my throat
Vomit spews across the table,
Guilty for what they have done.
Still a loose cable.

I J Clark

Baptism

she feels an angel that wears the
red-topped gleaming vanities, night-dress
besmirched with a witch's burnt bright lipstick,
inveigling the look of the gobsmacked.
trick-tease eyes reveal the mouth of a
down-trodden stake-burnt vixen with attitude:
this woman suits swearing well.

there is a boyfriend loves her bimbette fascination:
must be so, for a baby lies here
unearthed by the trowel of fornicated madness,
it blinks sleep and gapes troll-like
allegedly a hint of daddy.

a dowdiness of in-laws befalls the hospital room:
with a smoochiness she was bequeathed the sudden
breath. another for the litter, each one of the
howling brood announced late
in the very same room.
a swish of trees ignites the ignorer's cigarette below:
a cloud of daddy bursts in bangs on the bellowing
window, and the awkward hulk lays screeched.

outside the gulls, turning and gyring and tracing
the sea with plump stork beaks
drench the child in the spittle of a strange,
sad lager ritual:
it awaits like a medieval stench.

boyfriend burps, trees suck
his last cigarette and fall in seething gladness
into the hiss of pint-sized jars, mouth a teeth of giddiness
at what was pulled.
the baby cries.

Julie Ashpool

Bastard

'I want to be honest with you,'
He says, sincerity shining out of his eyes,
'You're still my first choice, even after all these years,
and I was just wondering if there might be a chance
we could, y'know, start again . . .?'

It's hard for her not to laugh.
Hard to believe, too, he could still imagine she might regret
the loss of him,
Could think she might be daft enough to wipe the slate clean
one more time.
She feels the old rage rise but fights it, stays cool,
maintains her dignity (and his)
tells him gently - sorry, not a chance,
and goes to bed depressed,
annoyed that she had let him tug her back into the past
so easily,
like an alligator drags its prey down into the swamp.

Then the phone call, just a few days later.
Her daughter spills the beans - he's getting married,
an American girl, he says.
She wonders why she is surprised.
He always had the knack of dodging failure,
just by reconsidering his options.
She thinks of his fiancée,
duped into believing she's his number one girl.

Bastard.

Pam Wardlaw

Change Arms

I used to be an octopus

cradling to my naked chest
a baby
wrapped and swaddled
as all the best babes are
and closing round him
the tentacles of arms
and dressing-gown
when we had gone down
at fourayem
to give his dam
some peace,
a gift of sleep,
to lie unworried.

And he, the babe,
would suck at his own splutters
and settle
and in tentacles of my love
rest flat and quiet

and we both knew wondrous peace.

That babe is now six foot three
and twenty-one and wise.
His wide-arm hug of greeting
makes me know
that he, now,
is the octopus.

Sean Jackson

Lovestruck

I swallowed you
unknowingly
a grain of wheat
a seed pearl

You grew inside me
in secret eggshell cradle
hidden
beneath your lashes

Carelessly
following moonlit pebbles
into the thicket of touching
fingers scorching

I wasn't able to run
when you startled me
with your ice-blue
luminosity

Gasping for shadows, spinning
into a burning flower
my blood
was lost in the snow

Stephanie Reise

In The Coliseum

Down there, where one is free to wander
and a half-starved simple woman
feeds the thousand cats the tourists like to pat,
a madman leans against the last restraining rail
and shouts.
Up here in the crumbled terraces
I cannot hear his words but I feel his passion
and I see the children laugh and the adults shy.
I have paid for a better view.
He doesn't belong in this circus;
he belongs in some family or some place
that knows his dangers and can quieten his fears.
I see him: a wild man calling on his gods, facing
the savage beasts in his head, weaving his arms
in a lonely fight which he cannot hope to win.
It's just like being back
home:
we have closed the wards;
we have closed our hearts;
we have thrown him to the lions.
Do I hear our rulers, our moneymen and, shame,
so many of our worthy citizens
all cheer?

Stephen Eric Smyth

Winter

I can sense Her,
gliding swiftly to arrive imminently.
The invisible messengers howling
heralding Her return.

The Queen of the year's depth
soon to resume Her throne,
in the midst of the heavy white carpet
under the glinting midnight lights.

Hostile to intrusions
She sharply guards Her domain,
banishing unwelcome trespassers
with the caress of an icy hand.

Her power will invade your life,
don't even try to fight.
When vulnerable and disarmed you sleep
in She whirls - midnight assault.

To awaken the next day
bones weakened near surrender,
the old and the frail tremble helplessly
the Queen is grasping their core.

She does not respond to worship
but survival demands preparation.
Honour the flickering flame of the heath
his loyal glow your only protection.

Alice Smyth

Music-Maker

A broadening white smile
Appears
Out of the smoke -
A white smile broadens
As the music begins
And the harp retells its story
Of an empty white land
That saw life when the first
Pure purple note began.

A flickering grey body
Dances
In the purple heat of the music -
A grey body dances
As the beat speaks
And the grey oboe begins its harmony
In the ever-echoing cave above the sky,
As the silver clouds twist and turn -
In time with the first blue shard of music.

A tapping foot
Rhythms
On the transparent case of the earth -
A foot rhythms
To the sound of simultaneity -
Existence emerging when the music begins;
The unity of grey music, twisting and turning
Until the return of the grey flickering body
To the white music of the silver clouds.

Alison Yarwood

Reality

In my Soul the Lotus of Compassion
unfurled her petals to rise above the surface
of disillusionment, discontent
I held him for a while before
he dropped into Oblivion
as substances from needle marks
and the emptying bottle of spirit
made marriage in his gut
until now the survivor
I thought of predators
feeding the weakness of their insecurity
by stealth from strength of the victim
sucking them dry to spit out
the seeds upon the pavement

his worldly goods a tired crumpled blanket
lay discarded in the doorway
as the tired crumpled body
lay discarded by the Spirit of the Sincere

a pace away a dog sat -
weeping love flowed free

his name - John
his epitaph
here lies a *real* person

Anita Richards

Reprise

Drunken nights and Monday mornings
Bargain booze and written warnings
Balding tyres and no tax disc
Kiss, don't tell - we'll take the risk

Autumn's dusk and summer's dawn
Footprints on the dewy lawn
Dodging every postman's knock
Watching, watching every clock

Missing minutes, stolen glances
Silent stares and cold advances
There's a life and love we could maybe share
Don't you know or don't you care?

You see . . .

There's more to life than pubs and bars
Take-away food and second-hand cars
There's a world outside this tiny town
There are thousands of colours other than brown.

There are roads that lead to different places
With different houses, streets and faces
There are other trees that elsewhere grow
You can climb them too, believe me, I know.

Annette P Beake

My Perfect Rose

At ten she came to me, three years ago,
There was 'something between us' even then;
Watching her write like Eliot every day,
Turn prose into haiku in ten minutes flat,
Write a poem in Greek three weeks from learning the alphabet,
Then translate it as 'Sun On A Tomb, Golden Place,
                              Small Sacred Horse.'
I never got over having her in the room of course, though
Every day she was impossible in a new way,
Stamping her foot like a naughty Enid Blyton child,
Shouting 'Poets don't do arithmetic!'
Or drawing caricatures of me in her book.

Then there were the 'moments if vision', her eyes
Dissolving the blank walls and made up faces,
Genius painfully going through her paces.
The skull she drew, the withered chrysanthemum
And scarlet rose, 'Decensus Averno', like virgil,
I supposed.

Now three years later, in nylons and tight skirt,
She returns from Grammar school to make a chaos of my room;
Plaiting a rose in her hair, I remember the words of her poem -
'For love is wrong/in word, in deed/but you will be mine'
And now her promise to come the last two days of term.
'But not tell them', the diamond bomb exploding
In her eyes, the key left 'accidentally' on my desk
And the faint surprise.

Barry Tebb

Misunderstood

Can you hear my screams
Over the deafening silence?
Nothing's been the same
Since everything changed.
I think I've been missing -
Since I found
Our platonic
Love affair.
It's very nearly always
Never the same.
But, I'd be a prisoner
If I escaped.
Do you think we can stay
The distance
Alone
Together?

Beth Winkworth

Dysfunctional . . .

she prefers
magnifying glasses:

she sees things closely really well -
picks me up on errors too trivial for me
to even bother correcting

and now,
having learned

a teaspoonful of Marx,
i see it's my turn . . .

but i prefer binoculars

and believe that i can see things reasonably well
with some distance

and when she asks me why her boss
is ordering her to cut labels from the garments that she sells

i explain to her
the basics of capitalism

and how it's designed to keep some people
in developed countries rich-rich

and the rest of the world
poor-poor

i explain to her how these garments were
most probably made from slave labour
in Hong Kong while she then sells them upmarket
for $1000 a piece in her boss's shop in Australia

and then i explain to her
who really pockets the big bicks

but tired of my analysis
she turns the conversation onto a different subject.

Brad Evans

Flight Path Of Friendship

*(To commemorate the meeting of the Luftwaffe Night Fighter Pilots
Association, and the Doncaster Branch of the RAF Air Gunners
Association in Laage, Germany, August 2000)*

Now friends, once enemies of old,
Of those days long ago, let their story be told.
How in darkness of night, they fought battles in the air,
The fighters and bombers, like the hound and the hare!

The knights of the air in their venomous steeds,
All responding in kind to their own nation's needs.
As the bombers droned overhead, lumbering, slow,
So the fighters would scramble, into battle they'd go!

Both sides had secrets, there was Oboe and Gee,
Würzburg and Freya helped the fighters to see!
So many were lost in those faraway years,
They remember them now, perhaps shed a few tears.

Tears born of memories of friends they once knew,
Brave men, comrades, with whom they once flew.
In aircraft whose names are now part of history,
Junkers and Messerschmitt, Lancaster, Whitley!

Now that war is long ended, those young men have grown old,
But we still can remember those whose story we've told.
The flightpath of friendship reaches out 'cross the sea,
Now they're all friends together, and that's how it should be.

Half a century's passed since our airmen took flight,
To do battle, now they laugh and tell tales in the night!
With a shake of the hand, and the smile of a friend,
Isn't that how all wars should end?

Brian L Porter

Moonlight Over The Fells

Dusk lies gently in the valley
Clothing silent fells with peace . . .
Eerie . . . the half-light of deepening sunset
Writes a new mystery play:
Bats and creatures of the night take their places
In another land,
Smoky curtains draw across fading fields,
Whisp'ring leaves and
Black waters watching with
Fathomless eyes . . .
Waiting to capture radiant stars
And grasp the lofty fells
As moonlight rises through
Ghostly, silver-tinged clouds
To bless the world
With a kiss,
A sparkling haze of
Diamond dew
Curling through the hedgerows and trees
In spectral forms beckoning
Skyward . . .
Moonlit figures of the night,
Yet, not of this world
They sweep the air
And scale the rising shadows
Of the crags
In the glorious pageant of
Moonlight over
The Fells . . .

Carolyn Smith

The Generation Gap

Acknowledging the difference
Dividing age from youth
Yet surely sometimes seeking
The same eternal truth?

We look at life together
Though often seem to see
With differing perspective
And act accordingly.

Facing the same problems
On impulse youth may act
While we may think experience
Calls for a little tact.

Despite the disappointments
And burdens we both bear
A vision of the future
We elders also share.

Though youth with all the answers
May find our ways too slow
In spite of our experience
How little we all know.

While youth must learn its lessons
And conquer its heartaches
We elders must be patient
Remembering our mistakes.

Although a timeless problem
Seeking the same end
A vision of the future
Youth and experience blend.

Cecil J Lewis

Woman

She passed me, long lean brown limbed
Black hair fell on her back
And the red cloth, two bands
On her moving body
Stirred like banners
As she walked

And as she turned, the line cut clean as a knife
The apple of her bottom
The twin perfection dazzled
And I heard the siren
Call to my dazed senses
And looked away

And the matron lady, seated and grey
Caught my gaze and held
In hers my eyes, held them
And the words that I heard
Unspoken spoke
In my heart

And her words, in the black skirt and white lace
Flat on her slack body
And the fat legs tucked beneath
In the sticky heat, were not
Shame on the body
You desire

They said something else, as her eyes held mine
Once I looked like that
You would not believe my breasts, my young bottom swung
And my legs supple as willows
Now I am this
And her too

Charles Evans

Black Trouble

She's dressed in black trouble, wide shadowed eyes
Enticing her double; the gooseberry mirror,
Impotent, grumbles 'You used to have eyes just for me.'

Her fishnet scent trails through the air,
Delicious, sublime; the air-freshener sniffs
'Lemon and pine no longer agree?'

And the sitting room's silently pleading
       'We really should talk - you and I.'
But her cocktail lips purse at the frowns of
Its sepia dressing-gown walls,
And the muttering kettle rumbles and shakes
As streetlight finally falls
Past the heavy grey curtain of comforting velvet denial:

'Can't you leave me alone?' she cries
'You just don't have what I want anymore
You still want to own me; well you *never* owned me!'

She slams the sullen front door
And whispers of steam drift like ghosts from the
Mouth of the kettle, abandoned unpoured.

Chris Sherlock

Sorrow

I stood on the edge of a cliff in the pouring rain,
The dark and the rain were all my sight would allow,
The cold and the wet were all I could feel.

Each droplet of rain carried a sad message
That reinforced the burden of my existence.
I was drenched in grief; I had become paralysed with sorrow;
I fell to my knees and cried with the rain.

I watched my spirit fall from my body;
My eyes followed the innocence of my inner child, as a part of
me died.
Each new teardrop relived a memory of how distress had
become my world.
I looked to the skies and asked for just one moment of peace
To show my soul that I am more than anguish.

Christine Nicholson

The Garden Before Rain

White crescendo.
The swan sedate
on dry land.

Daffodils throb heady yellow.

Muffled tread small twigs
among insignificant grasses,
heather-rattle,
stones muted grey, black
brick-brown.

The quaint polyphony of ducks
echoes like axe-blows
of distant quarry men.

Furious, the beat of wings.

A February chestnut leans aged arms
into dark green water,
lifts them
at an angry sky.

Dal Strutt

Sophie

Upon a billboard,
Advertising perfume
Is a picture of a lady,
Naked as the day she was born,
Wearing nothing save for shoes.
There is an aura that she is
Confident with her firm body,
Indeed, there is a hint of enjoyment
As she caresses her left breast,
As if awaiting to share that enjoyment
With someone else.

But the stiff-necked
And narrow nosed
Rose up shouting comments;
'Disgusting, Obscene
Unclean, Lewd, Degrading',
Until weak-willed officials removed
The advertisement from the billboards.

How strange that those who condemned
Have forgotten that we are formed in
The Image of God.

David A Garside

Fighting Back

I was born wearing your boxing gloves
You told me I was a fighter
I had Daddy's hands you said
Daddy's hands to guide the future

And you challenged me in a boxing ring
As I was just learning to stand
You told me I was born to fight
To live my life in public light

Daddy's hands held all the plans
But they pushed me over the ropes
You pushed, I surrendered
You watched me choke

You drowned me in your training shoes
With Daddy's feet I could never lose
And you held me much too close to you

You squashed me in your top left pocket
I saw your eyes flee their sockets
Daddy, you could not see straight
Daddy could not see his fate

And you stuffed me in your boxing pants
I thumped and punched
And I fought with your hands
Daddy's hands, Daddy's plans

I can punch but not defeat your grasp
When will I triumph over years gone past?
When will I break from your tight belt
To make you feel what I have felt?

Denise Stock

Home And Away

Down, down, far below,
From the bowels of the earth so it seems,
Next door's generator grinds its way,
A thousand drills digging up the road
In the distance.
A labour of holes, breaking barriers of sound
At midnight.

Whereas, at break of day,
The washing machine
Screams its welcome at
A new morning just about to break,
Dwarfing birdsong
In its claims of territory.
While above, my bed couch
Lies uneasy.

Like drifting incense
To an alien god,
Poison smoke arises
Through the flimsy slats
Of wood and plaster,
And bathes my bed in sacrifice.

She is awake to greet the day
In scents of Raleigh leaf,
Anointed nicotine,
High Priestess of the morn
Hails the new dawn
With drudgery.

> *Diane Burrow*

Paper Dreams

Another rainy day,
As I pass by she's there again,
Hands frozen, voice broken,
As she shouts for her pennies;
Paper words to sell,
Paper dreams to build,
A world to tell
But no one who'll listen;
They mostly walk by,
No time, no money, no care,
How dare she stand there and make them aware!
But she doesn't curse,
Just a thank you and smile
And she's still there in the wind and the rain,
With her paper words to sell
And paper dreams to build;
Maybe next year
The smile will be wider,
The hands will be warmer,
A few pounds the richer
And the paper words will be memories,
The paper dreams will become stone,
Perhaps then she'll have a future,
Then she'll have a home.

Donna Llewellyn-Kear

She Sleeps In My Heart

She was a lady
that was strong
yet gentle

At times an
absolute fire-breathing
dragon
but she was also
funky and experimental

I remember watching
when I was small
as she chose to create new shoes
with
green gloss paint

She wore these shoes
and with afro-esque hairdo
and red lipstick
hit the road

The night she died
I was surprisingly calm
yet somehow hysterical
her breathing was shallow
the choices were sealed

I closed her eyes
after she'd taken the
last breath
and her hand slipped from mine

I used to wonder if
she loved me
but I love her
and that is enough
I let her go
and I was still
as she embraced
death

I let her go
but she sleeps in my heart

Dorina Shannon

Pagan Dance

Who shall forget their frantic dancing,
Who shall forget, who once shall see
Slaves of the serpent goddess prancing
Wildly round the sacred tree?

Hands entwining, faces shining,
Crazed by an eternal pining,
Never sated, driven silly
By the scent of jungle-lily;
Long ago the roots have rotted,
Still they caper, still besotted,
Servants in the cause of wrong,
Chanting an unearthly song.

Apples gleaming, fairest-seeming,
Fruit is only fit for dreaming,
Heaven juice is not for tasting
Though the lips be slowly wasting,
Feet must tread the fatal measure,
Keep the narrow path of pleasure,
Pacing faster, ever faster,
To the music of disaster.

Glutton leaves swell and shimmer,
Though the moonlight waxes dimmer,
Still the dance is not withdrawn,
Desperation seeks no dawn,
Noon nor evening can bring rest
Nor solace to a soul possessed,
And one who strayed, in secret thought,
Returns, and dances now, distraught.

He may not sleep, nor even weep,
Must ever constant rhythm keep,
Never daring once to droop
Lest the birds of death should swoop,
All his reason subtly riven
From his mind as he is driven
To preserve her falsity,
Who sold him into sorcery.

Who shall forget their frantic dancing,
Who shall forget, who once shall see
Slaves of the serpent goddess prancing
Wildly round the sacred tree?

Dorothy Buyers

A Glint Of Moonlight

(To the memory of Horiana Escalona de Del Rio)

Begin dear piano your epitaph
Of gleaming ivory symphony
Awake her image that I miss
Lifting this mourning mist
Let my longing heart to be drawn
To her bosom where I was born

Bitter-sweet chords accompanying
My Thursdays and Sundays mass
Unfold her face . . . her eyes
Her unforgettable smile . . .
The soft touch of her hands
Her life . . . that once was mine

Oh glint of crescent moon!
Pearliness, suspended up high
Cradling memories of her love
From a deep-blue starry sky
Descending through the vitreauxs
To the stillness of my mind

Oh spheres of enchanting notes!
Connecting rainbow to my birth
Ethereal, swift, like snowflakes
Whitest dreams of yesterday
When she held me in her arms
Hoping that I would forever stay

Memories that I live and re-live
Of my longing days with her
When she was my muse and my guide
. . . Of that infant wonderland

A whisper of her golden hair
Wafts, as a secret on the wind
The hues of today's tranquil moon
Bring her kisses that I need
Oh lips grazing my forehead!
. . . Hands stroking my hair
Mouth that has beckoned my name
In a song that will always remain

Oh mother . . . beloved mother!
I dearly miss those tender days
Days in which we laughed, sang, played,
. . . Ohh, your beautiful face
And your eyes! . . of serene sea
That bathed me, lovingly

I've held you since then, and forever
Embracing the wonder of you
Floating in notes of a piano
Rapture in glinting of moons
Where saints watch all over us
In sleeping sacred domes

Eduardo Del-Rio Escalona

Flora In Winter

The contractor's daughter,
a beautiful Russian girl,
came to see him.

Her pale, snow-covered
puffball coat melted
into the dust of walls falling.

We ask her to stand
in the doorway of
the demolished apartment.

And fill her arms with branches
and budded twigs
encased in ice.

And with a bouquet frozen at the window.
Melting
darts roil the dirt.

Grow to wobbly carbuncles
test the slant
break free.

A rivulet forms, a stream
rushes the stairs,
waterfalls through the balusters.

And our winter Flora
renews, refreshes, beneficent
as her namesake, Spring.

Ellen Peckham

A Dark Paradise

(For Alan)

A ghost from the past - you dance through my dreams,
haunt waking moments - deprive me of sleep;
And our love is only kept alive
from a place in my heart and inside my mind.
A sky with no heaven above it
I lie here beneath - frozen in time,
memories to keep.
Dancing beneath the moon - you became my vice
leading the way to a dark paradise.
Stars were like promises in the sky,
Bright lights of hope - illusion or lies?
And so to my heart you laid down your claim,
dancing together in sweet summer rain.
Pushing the limits over the edge,
you stole me away and into your bed.
Your lips touched mine
and you breathed new life into me,
kindled my spirit and touched my soul;
Opened my eyes and reawakened me -
for a short while you made me whole.
You were my King and I was your Queen.
I was in love and you were my sin.
But now our castle has come tumbling down
all that I ask is lay down your crown.
Four seasons have come - four seasons have gone -
And for seasons I have been alone;
And still in the night
You dance through my dreams,
A vision of love,
A dove with clipped wings.

Emma Clifton

Washing Up

You crossed my mind
not walking almost dancing.
Leaving ugly footprints on my brain,
making a pattern -
an arrangement of
evocative performance -
the inculcation of
dependency on you.

You raid my space
with torment and derision,
challenging my new-found liberty.
Preserve the tradition -
an agreement of
subordinate position
I have reclaimed myself
and you have gone.

I will forget
the part that I was playing,
the mise-en-scène has now been rearranged.
My new composition -
of achievement and
assertive disposition;
my identity reborn
without apology.

Eve Warner-Howard

A Secret Place

I know of a secret place.
Where sunbeams dance across my face
Through leafy trees, where bluebells grow
And wood anemones, like drifts of snow.

A place that's quiet and so serene
Where I can sit and dream and dream.
The wood pigeon's there and the blue barred jay
And I can while my time away.

Clear water tumbles in the shallow brook,
The raucous voice of the widowed weeds rook.
I know of a secret place
Where sunbeams dance across my face.

Flora Denning

I Remember, One Summer

I remember the fir trees at the end of the garden,
Deep green centre branches bathed in sun rays
Their tips a silver and yellow bright with light,
And pink honeysuckle with pungent perfume
Had entwined itself around a higher branch.

I saw you there, pausing in play, to stand and gaze
Fair-haired child caught up in a world of wonder
Lost to adults, the land where the very young dwell.
Blue T-shirt, red pants, hands held out in delight
Thinking with the mind and feeling with the heart
Part of that enchanted pool at peace with nature.

Shadows spreading from the fir trees
Your shadow arms outstretched in movement.
Secure warm, you turned and ran across the lawn
protected by your childhood.
I remember you there, thinking with the mind
Feeling with the heart and reaching to the light,
In the land where the very young dwell.

Freda Grieve

Aurelia's Hands

I must remember: onions.
Milk, ground almonds
and a light bulb. To replace
that bad-tempered one next to my
head at night. It flickers
moodily and leaves me staring
at the blazing ceiling
like an irritated moth.

A thumbnail, carefully
manicured, traces nicks
in the wooden tabletop, digging up
the greasy debris of past breakfasts
and staged Sunday lunches.
The amplified whirr of the hot wash
hauls me back into daytime
television sadness and

outside, in the mad, unruly
crimson air, a powdery cardigan
flaps its ice-blue tunnel-wings
as if to save the windfall from mouldering.

Gabriela Mauch

Butterflies Have No Wings

I have watched this butterfly,
Dancing in the shade.
Her wings fluttering cautiously
In the palm of my hand.

Such beauty is bewitching,
Colours divine; so light!
Intricately sketched and
Painted masterfully
By the skilful flick, of her artist's brush.

I have longed for my skin to absorb her shadow
As my lips are left stained,
From our last impulsive kiss.

'Twas in you, I found her;
A butterfly without wings, delicate and proud.

Through you, I was left with supreme colours
That circled my mind and clouded my eyes.

'Twas in you, I would confide
And feel my heart slowly lift,
Followed by the flicker of your smile.

I remember you once said to me,
That if you were my Confessor
Then all would be forgiven.

But, Father Cardinal,
I have nothing to confess.

Gazala Rashid

Looms

The spider seems to think that I
Have come to kill her seventh eye
She hovers in the corner crack
My wanton breathing on her back.

Nowhere to turn, no web to lie
Her sisters in the garden cry
No fly to feast, no place to run
You rattle but your weaving's done.

Give up your crown - you dare be queen
Yet even as I watch you preen
My fist would be the ident's ton,
Go splatter legs the spider spun.

But how could I besmirch your form
And end the kitting of your haulm
Slink into dark and climb the ray
To tanglement of other days.

Graeme Vine

The Love That Dare Not Speak Its Name

He knew it was all over.
They had caught him at last -
All his witty epigrams,
His clever verbal cut and thrust,
Defeated at last
By leaden-footed logic,
Statements,
Hard-headed facts.
Here there could be no space
For whimsy and play.
This was their territory.
They had him now.
And so he played his finest part -
The tragic hero.
They had never seen him
In this role before.
It was a new experience.
But they were silent
As he spoke.
They did not laugh.
He played it out so well,
Telling of love that dare not speak its name.
And there was brief silence,
Until applause broke out.
Quite wonderful it was -
So moving.
They did not see that he had dropped
His mask.

Jackie Lapidge

Drowned Her

She swam in on the early tide
rotten to the core
a raft for gulls
naked and ashamed
she wrapped herself in seaweed
lay in a huddle
in a pool beyond the shoreline.

She moves slowly
through still waters
wrapped up in leaves
all her fingers reach to me
and I swoop down
to run my fingers
through her hair.
She smiles in ripples
and if it weren't for the drowning
we'd hold hands.

James Noonan

Forever Winter

Drip, drip, drip, went the tap,
She could not afford to mend.
Drip, drip, drip, ran her tears,
Slipping down from her chin.
Bills piled high on the dresser.
Despair sitting next to decay.
The clock in the dining room ticking,
Why stay?
She hauled her bent frame into action.
From the threadbare and grubby armchair.
Shoved her poor painful feet into slippers
Full of holes, fraying from wear.
She shuffled her way to the kitchen.
Attempted to muster a smile.
At the well-used before lonely teabag,
That had served her a while.
Or perhaps spoil herself from her stock-pile
Cordon Bleu or Egon Ronay?
No, a half crumbled cube of Bovril,
Was her luxurious treat for the day.
In the corner, a mangy old moggy,
Who like her had seen better days.
Raised one eye from his slumbering stupor.
Fixed her in his gaze.
Rubbed his tail round her legs with affection,
As she shared her last crust of bread.
Would anyone really notice,
If tomorrow they both were found dead?

Janice L Williams

Continuity

There's a gravestone in our churchyard
That has passed the test of time -
Its words are hardly visible
Beneath the years of grime,
But I sometimes pause and ponder
On that sacred spot alone
And read the moving message
Inscribed upon that stone.
It mourns the leading singer
Of the choir of bygone years,
And, as I read those loving words,
I brush away a tear.
'Sleep undisturbed' the message reads
'Beneath thy sacred shrine,
'Til Angel voices waken thee,
With notes as sweet as thine.'
Oft, when our choir assembles,
And files through Vestry door,
I seem to hear the quiet tread
Of Choristers before.
I hear their distant voices,
Raised with one sweet accord.
Enhancing all the worship
Of Jesus Christ Our Lord.

Joan Leahy

Cast A Dark Shadow

In the pale eye of dawn lies
a long dark shadow.
Somewhere, a child cries. Somewhere,
beneath the debris of war,
a child lies. Somewhere, a hand
reaches out. Somewhere, a child dies.

In the pale eye of dawn lies
a long dark shadow.
Somewhere, a siren calls. Somewhere,
beneath the underbelly of war,
a bomb falls. Somewhere, a man
voices an order. Somewhere, a man dies.

And in the pale eye of the world lies
a long dark shadow.
Somewhere, war casts a long dark
shadow of death, of destruction,
of annihilation, of anger: of fear. And
somewhere a child cries and somewhere
a child dies: until somewhere an eye
shifts focus and a hand reaches out for peace.

Jocelyn McKinnon

Isle Of Ewe

She tugged an earlobe
and pointed through the rivulets of rain,
beyond the glass
that separated us
from the saturated atmosphere outside.
Playing her word game
and grinning at her cleverness,
she waited for my penny to drop
like sugar cubes
into my second cup of tepid tea.

My thoughts, a troubled bobbing bird
adrift on the heavy, sky-replenished sea,
I looked across the loch
to where the arc of a gannet
transected the line
contrived by her outstretched splintered nail,
and understood.

Straining, protected pines held their lines
on a hummock of the misted, near horizon.
Isle of Ewe.
I turned to see her mouth the words
and knew I must return the silent
affirmation with a smile.

John Tirebuck

A Soldier Lost

Dawn had risen, without remorse.
Fog lay coarse, like a plague of ghosts amongst the dead.
The skylight turned hazel beyond that lost satin blue.
My heyday far from these lines, far from this life.
Silent, silent.
The tapestries of screams dormant to gun fire.
This graveyard of clay, barbaric massacre.
If I could touch my rose once more before my final rest.
Never let your petals fall for this is not goodbye.
As I look upon the butter-corn gold of the rising sun,
The shrapnel draws me bitterly cold.
I hear a voice,
faint is the calling of my name.
Fading, fading,
Faded.

Jolene Neary

The Hawk

Wings snickering a silent hum,
A rising, falling pendulum,
The meadow waits, silent and numb.

The lone hawk assassin scutters
Mid thermals pulsating, putters,
Below fear frozen prey flutters.

Stiffened against Earth's stoic mound
She watches panting on the ground
And listens for a sudden sound.

His leaden weight drops from the skies
As nature's arrow-dart, he dives,
A whiplash knot slips from her eyes.

Removes the fear within her chest,
Her fight for life is put to rest,
And lives to take another test.

Wings snickering a silent hum,
A rising, falling pendulum,
The meadow still waits, always numb.

Josephine Duthie

Children's Cemetery

The rows of crosses hit me hard
Walking through the cemetery yard
Ornate angels perched on high
Seemed, like me, to wonder why.

Strange stillness filled the crisp, clear day
As I sought the place where Megan lay
So many crosses, so many tears
This grief will live for untold years.

My gift I clutch in my left hand
Until, at last, arrived, I stand.
I struggle to picture your tiny face
Lying at rest in this quiet place.

My eyes search the names on the crosses nearby
The unknown friends with whom you lie
So many, so small, the tears now flow
Abruptly, I turn and go.

My friend, for you I can only weep
For the child you only saw in sleep.
The small hand in mine is no longer enough
I scoop up my child, enfold him with love.

Julie C Ashton

Montserrat Caballé In 'Salome'

The desperate beauty of your voice,
Your anguished stoop,
Your arms outstretched,
Despairing, to cradle that head,
Controlling your fury
Of wild distress.
The music, a long-drawn sorrow,
Passionate with regret.
The long loss of hope,
The smooth, shrill,
Soaring, swooning voice,
Too fatal, too final, too late.
Never, never, now not ever
Can you relent, ever
Your revenge forget,
How can this aching misery,
This desperate fury
Such beauty beget.

Kathleen Goodwin

Addiction

The hit, the high, the
nicotine buzz,
Adrenaline rush, Queen of the World.
You took away my youth.

The wow, the wham, the
chemical sting,
Confidence burst, Princess of Power.
You took away my health.

The pow, the brash, the
nicotine stab,
Fatal grip, Demon of the Damned.
You took away my mother.

Kay Jude

The Soulless Lair

The stench of this horned viper,
The rhyming
Of her soulless lair,
The meagreness
Of the taunting,
Daunts the debonair,
And makes hard his heart.

Her skill in persuasion,
Could haunt the millionaire,
'Til bankrupt, he swears,
The die-hard gaol,
Will not suck his marrow,
And grapples with the machine
That swears an oath to poverty.

Kerri Moore

The Beast Of Zion

Scattered victims of this war
Their bodies limp and still
Yet of their blood the beast of Zion
Has not drunk his fill

The stench of death upon his breath
And cruelty in his eyes
Between his teeth are innocents
He feasted on their cries

Flesh torn in a frenzy
From the bullets that he spat
Palestinian children murdered,
Cameras witnessed that

A beast without a conscience
Dripping acid from his tongue
To be cut, when he's defeated
And then rolled in his own dung.

Kim Montia

Lawrence

My grandfather claimed, each time we came to visit,
that I would eat him out of house and home.
I was a chubby child and it probably would have been true,
had he lived a few more years,
but he didn't. He left an old woman all alone,
and a young one missing the obligatory tears.

I grew up thinking that when I was big,
I would do as my older brothers and sisters did,
which was take it as a joke, when he said,
'There's no more room in the inn today.'
But anyway he did not live, for me to tell him,
that I thought him a grumpy old man who I'd rather dead.

And maybe I was sorry that I drove my scooter into his trouser leg,
or that the little springy green men made so much noise,
but did it have to be a sin to not say good night to you
before I went to bed,
or make a mess with the toys.

I was just a kid. And anyway you never took me fishing,
or to the races, and I knew you took my dad.
So you can't have been surprised that amongst all those faces,
I was the one who thought I'd have to slam my hand in a car door
or something, to make me sad.

And there must have been something,
because my gran read a leaflet on God
And did not go to bed that night.
And Dad sobbed, which is still only the second time
I've seen him do that in my life.

And Dad said something about before the rot setting in,
Was I part of that rot?
Your professional football playing days would have been
somewhere to begin,
or the war. Not a lot. But something for you to know
I was listening.

It falls on deaf ears now, but I think of you to squishy crocodiles,
and when there's no-one to tell Gran that it's number round time,
and when she puts number four on the horses, once in a while,
because you never approved of gambling. So I wasn't blind.

But I never did get it. Until yesterday.
Taking that 'All Sorts' book off the shelf.
The one with your 'Alan Turner' poem in.
Your way. My way.

Laurie Anderson

Cycle Of Viciousness

In vein,
He tries.

The papery thinness of news,
Envelops him on a bed of corrugation.
As sleep the only recluse,
Solitude to his destitute ways.
Copper brings the liquid and a paradise,
Of bruises and saliva:
Salvation in a twisted sense.
Brought to the downtrodden state
Unable to replenish pride.

In vein,
He tries,
He tried.

Leigh Sandilands

By The Water Tower

(Burton-On-Trent, Staffordshire)

High on the hill lies a place of solitude
Where the heavens open to shed its light
The tranquil setting lets me fade away
Lifting my troubles and woes
The distance seems so far away
I sit and close my eyes
The still atmosphere engulfs me
Spreading its wings to take me away
The cool breeze blows across my face
The green fields are so far, yet so close
My old high school sits on the hill in the distance
Where memories come flooding back
I see a train speeding across the distant bridge
Placing movement into this picturesque
As the trees blow and begin to whisper
I drift back to reality once more
I look up at the tower, looming over me
I begin to move and walk away
Out of focus, out of sight
This place will always be here
For me to escape from life's blues.

Lindsey Knowles

Quietude

Yes, I saw the sudden scurry of yellowed
leaves fluttering to the ground,
watched the geraniums being lifted safely
for the coming spring.
Now, with fire smoke drifting uneasily
across the windless garden,
a calm prevails.

The earth is settling
for a period of waiting.

Louise Rogers

Kismet

The ayes, the noes, the these, the those,
The opens, shuts, the ifs, the buts,
The hopes, the doubts, the ins, the outs,
Philosophy?
You and me.
Illusions, dreams, ambitions, schemes,
Quick-quick, slow-slow, stay put or go,
Flying high, sinking low,
Apathy?
You and me.
The ups, the downs, Shakespeare's clowns,
The morning rush, the evening hush,
The groans, the grins, the losses, the wins,
Reality?
You and me.
The tears, the mirth, Heaven on Earth,
The hits, the misses, the fights, the kisses,
The do's, the don'ts, the wills, the wont's,
Stupidity?
You and me.
The pride, the shame, the power game,
The stand or surrender, the rough, the tender,
The playful tweak, the spiteful streak,
Uncertainty?
You and me.
The nearness, the distance, the pièce de resistance,
The turn of a lock, the tick of a clock,
The loving, the hating, the longing, the waiting,
Insanity?
You and me.
The only one in a crowd the other would see . . .

M Patricia Churchill

The Victim

I do not recollect your name in
This lost era of darkened time, no doubt
I may have known you well, your touch and
Gentle face come - faint recall - through spates of
Weariness and confused thought, in knots of
Anxious moments, in fearing you are gone.

You draw a cordon round disordered days,
Hold me from failing every childish
Task, while I, crouched low in my numb-mind ways
Within this harrowing space of wasting
Silence, strive to reach out, touch, unearth, a
Token that converts all dark despair to
Reason; transcending loneliness and fear.

Yet, in these bounds of darkness a warmth, I
own, binds and sustains me;
The name is love.

Margret Phillips

Victoria's Grave

(For Jane, my daughter)

The burned-out car,
The dead note,
The suicide of earthly love,
The crucifixion of anon
And love most cruel crying in the wind,
I leave her now to heaven
And pray for her channel of peace.

I can no longer find you,
Your face lost in gnarled trees
Hidden when the moon turned black
Your body lying in dead earth,
The dreaming gone
And me dying too
On that funeral-kind of day.

Your peace is perfect,
Mine is not . . .

Margarette Phillips

The Road

The tarmac artery pulses.
Congested traffic cells clot and gush.
White platelets divide, steering a safer course
always moving
always pounding
along the road.

Bent grey rails sprout floral tributes.
Damp papers, faded crepe, heads bowed
The saddest of perennials hang
precarious witnesses to life cut short.

Ink drips as skies cry.
Written kisses melt over time.
Time the great healer - the greatest deceiver
drives along its interminable route.

The pain softens
the road remains hard.

Mark R Briggs

Last Drop

You pour me another brandy
You encourage me to drink
Not to take advantage of me
But to drown my sex I think

We don't speak about the subject
It's easier without the rows
But my urge is getting even stronger
And I feel shackled by my vows

As we watch another movie
Solemnly slumped on the settee
I get turned on by every screen kiss
And scream inside: Why not me?

You pour me another brandy
I watch you, love you still
But hate is creeping ever closer
Preparing for the final kill

You drain the last drop from the bottle
Romance, sex and passion dead
Sadly drunk I say: Goodnight love
And lay awake in the spare bed.

Miranda Rook

The First Grand-Daughter

Hair bracken brown
silk fronds new bonded,
eyes pellucid, show
every day new-born.
Small teeth delineate
a smile of utter pleasure,
hands still flutter
but the grasp is sure.
Learning to give
touch infinitely gentle,
her disposition stretches
sweetly from her,
radiance
greets her mother.

Monica Redhead

Little Girl

Hey little girl
With far away eyes.
What are you thinking
When you look to the skies.
Are you wishing the grass under your feet
The feel of it
A treasure to keep
Are you wishing the wind in your hair
As you run around and play.
Are you wishing today of all days
You could be like other children
On this your birthday.
Oh little girl of mine
I would give all I be
To see you running around
Happy and free.
Free of the wheelchair
Legs in motion
Walking one step at a time.
Miracles do happen, we are told.
So Lord if you are looking down
Grant her. Her wishes
If only in her dreams.

Moyna Bond

Webs

Beautiful death traps wreathed in moisture
from an early autumn dew.
Lovely patterns strung impossibly
catching and reflecting light of every hue.

Too wet for the spider yet to use them,
near to breaking by the weight of water.
Yet dried up shells of the once living hang
as mute testimony to the slaughter.

What a miracle of life and death so closely
interwoven and juxtaposed.
There is no quarter can be asked or given,
just life as it is in the raw - exposed.

Neil Hardy

Strange Shoes

Brown eyes open in wonder
as I told you stories
while you sat upon my knee . . .
Now I stare at you in wonder . . .
Gone the fat little legs
running around the garden
chasing ducks and hens
and hiding in home-made dens
always a bruised forehead from
too many falls off your bicycle . . .
Now you have long skinny legs
that dance the night away
in enormous strange shoes
balanced by unusually weird
yet somehow fascinating hairstyles . . .
I watch in amazement
and admire all your braveness
                    that I never had . . .
You zoom through your young life
in carefree haste busily collecting
tattoos and assorted friends along the way . . .
Brown eyes wide open in wonder . . .
Now covered in fancy make-up
Now covered in complicated plans
                    and important ideas
You never seem to show any fears . . .
Brown eyes wide open in wonder . . .

Netta Irvine

Beside Still Waters

(For Jenny Owen)

Deep within my impassioned heart; is where I held you;
Whilst we were far apart.

And I looked for you, beside still waters;
Reflected in the peaceful scene.
I heard your whispering voice, in the twilight breeze;
And its soft expression, in a star kissed stream.

We shared this breath of summer's morning;
Cool glistening dew upon the grass.
Our hands brushed lightly, sensually together:
We prayed our love would last . . . and last.

We stared into the stars of Heaven . . . I saw them captive in your eyes.
Your soul and mine combined together; sublime;
Beyond all boundaries of space, and time.

I looked for you in leafy woodlands . . . sensed your free spirit
in the pine.
A fleeting glimpse of intense pleasure . . . a moment so divine.

And in that silent solitude, I came upon a rose.
Its fragile petals, I cupped lightly; its fragrant scent; held me in repose.
As with whispered breath, and eyes gently closed,
I touched upon your trembling lips, a soft and delicate, tender kiss.
Our covenant to become as one . . . 'soulmates':
Love's priceless gift; conceived within a moment; of eternal bliss.

Holding hands with the stars, we felt the thrill of pure love's delight.
As passion took out entranced spirits, on their first celestial flight.
I held your heart . . . you held me tight . . . enchanted lovers . . .
Or was it all:
Just an essence of a wistful dream.
Echoed mirrored colours, of this soul's endless searching . . .
As I looked for you . . . 'Beside Still Waters.'

Nigel Gatiss

Daughter Of Eve

O yielding daughter of Eve, why allow such torment?
To give of yourself so freely and yet take little for sustenance.
You cannot live from love alone, you need to grow and flourish
Do not resign yourself to mere existence, for you are Mightier than any
Adam and healthier of heart.
Spread your crushed roots and allow yourself to expand and rise.

You suffocate yourself to allow others to breathe and prosper,
Denying them nothing which you are able to sacrifice.
Your soul is bright, lucid and pure of heart
Your branches protect all those that gather beneath them
And you shelter all those who selfishly form there.

You bear the fruits of your labour for all to feast upon and yet
You do not take any nourishment for yourself.
You permeate warmth and comfort others and yet
You do not take any warmth in comfort for yourself.

Do not wither by denying your true self,
Allow your inner strength to uplift you and allow you to bloom.
You are beautiful and beautiful things need to grow.

Nina Haime

Black Magnificat

A halting journey -
    for the most part uncharted -
        fuelled by vine-shrivelled fruit,
by insipid springs
    quenching absolutely nothing
    while my cup gathers dust.

I'm driven from within,
    driven to the edge and beyond
        to an abysmal descent:
snaking torchlights
    spiral into the canyon
        leading me to the den

where - pinned in the dark -
    I falter in the heat of
        her snarling incense.
Yet this is no hunt;
    my stuttering enchantments
        seem to soothe the injured beast.

The trust builds slowly,
    tangles of wire removed,
        sores cleaned and poulticed,
as, deep in that dank cave
    my own injury risking,
        devotedly I serve.

With this dire consequence:
    the healing of the Panther.

    The sinews of my soul
are taut with her knowing;
    when I rise from the canyon,
    I am haunted
by her scent, the sudden
    pounce of her passion.

In the valley of the shadow
there is fear, and there is no fear.
For again she is with us:

so dark . . . so magnificent.

Nora Leonard

Ignorant Desire

Your green-banked river
forms again and flows.
I water at a hole
where no grass grows

and in that thirsting
fever grope your land
only to find parched bones
in dust and sand.

You have a self
my needless self could know,
but through my ignorant
desire you go

a mere ghost of possession.
Which is true?
Need of your body
disembodies you.

Norman Buller

In Flanders Fields

now
there are roses
around headstones
row after row
in peaceful
immaculate gardens
birds sing
over old frontiers
the quarrel was great
and down that
stalemate sluice
poured youth

now
diminishing remembrance
families pass on
medals old photographs
lying around
names unknown
fired with that torch
not one thought
twenty years on
history would repeat
in Flanders fields

Oliver Main

The Vigil

Green shoots sprout in the black earth
Their thread white roots unseen.
Her fingers are blue and cold,
She stands in the doorway, waving
Not calling goodbye, saving
Her breath for the lonely night
And the wait for light.

The walls close in, their faces
Stare, smile, keeping her company
In the vigil till morning.
Night shrouds the garden.
Pewter mists envelop yew and ash,
Dulling the shadowless mass,
Lifeless and still, waiting for dawn
To caress the wet black boughs,
The sodden lawn.

Framed in the kitchen window
She stares, glazed and spent
Surrounded by darkness.
She seems so slight, this ancient being,
Whose life is all but spent,
Her cup in hand, she climbs the stair
Knowing that dawn is almost here
And her vigil is ended.

Pat Coldwell

The Deserted Village

Surprisingly in dignity and calm,
Like Queen of Scots, bare-necked as axe arched high,
She waits in silent patience without qualm,
My now deserted village in the sky.

Blind windows now no longer scan the view,
With detonators waiting for their spark.
Expert technicians in the wrecking crew
Scoff hope with which she grew up tall and stark.

For early on, with newly painted foyer,
With lifts that whisked young loves to dizzy heights
The tower nursed new life, a loving voyeur
Of upward aspirations hopeful flights.

But plastic bags, discarded, swirled round,
Graffiti's senseless daubs besmirched her walls:
And urine-stenching lifts would all resound
To ribald, loud-mouthed, vacant-minded vandals.

The decent, good, the old, the frail, defeated,
Withdrew behind five-levered locks, suspicious
That human jungle hunters roamed, conceited
Around their landings, corridors, malicious.

So year on year, the Tower's very essence,
Her concrete, glass, her broken underclasses
By daily inches crept in evanescence,
Disintegrating with herself, her huddled masses.

Her execution warrant now is signed for.
'Damn you!', 'At last good riddance!' scream the banners.
But thinkers know she did as was designed for . . .
So don't condemn the village . . . *blame the planners!*

Patrick Brady

Victorian Scene

The hansom slid, slipped, slithered away, wheels
Crushing the soft snow, soundlessly; she stood,
Shivering, not entirely due to cold.

She knew, he had left something of himself
Behind, sure of that, but too soon to feel
The flutter-kick. That would come later on.

Certain, she knew, he left behind a jewel,
A thing precious from him, but burden too
For her. The loss of job, of family,
She would not consider; she had been his
For eternity in a few moments.
Now her loneliness; now she watched as that,
That cold cab crushing the uncomplaining
Snow, slow-moving over the icy ground
Took him with it, and inside him the piece
Of her that never would return.

Paul A Reeves

The Apple Tree

We spent many long hours in your shadow,
Two boys turning soil in Grandad's back garden.
We searched for spent cases from the Battle of Britain
Brass, fallen from the skies and through
Your budding fingertips as you grew.
We beat rusty nails through
Your skin, building our camps
Against your coarse flesh
As you protected us.
I'd climb the rope ladder into your arms, and
The Germans hiding in
Nan's house
Never saw me at all.
Safe, we played, until High Command
Withdrew us from the battle.
Called in, mosquito-bitten,
We feasted on rations
Of milk and custard creams.

Years later, a storm finally felled you
And they came and took you away,
Before this old soldier could
Say goodbye.

Paul Edwards

Comic Relief

Nightly, he plays
the gallery.
Jack the Lad.
Secreting feelings
'neath the quips
and cheery banter.
Performing through
an alcoholic haze.

Daily, he despairs,
yearning to prise,
that mask off,
reveal his inner self.
Expose that silent
desperation, which lies
beyond the wisecracks
and the jokes.

Hourly, he succumbs,
sipping at the whisky,
always close to hand.
Letting thoughts of money,
diminish his resolve.
Staggering fitfully towards
those glaring footlights.
Lured by the laughter
of others.

Paul Kelly

Ivory Tower

(This poem is of the dictator,
seen all over the world)

Human life, can't mean a thing,
to the man, who would be king.
Sitting in his ivory tower,
thinking how to gain more power.
Henchmen always by his side
those against him, mostly died.
Woman, man and even child,
makes no difference, all defiled,
broken by his mad desire
to reach the top and go much higher.
Land and money, is his need,
to feed his craving, to feed his greed.
Trampling on those in his way,
terrorising day by day.
Killing, torture, to those in fear,
he doesn't care, doesn't want to hear.
Getting richer, by the hour,
living in his ivory tower.

Peter Jessop

Firstborn

I remember when I first held you, and looked into your eyes,
I promised you then that my love would never die.
The years, they passed so quickly, or at least to me it seemed,
And soon memories of your childhood were just a colourful dream.
Then you started changing, but it wasn't for the best
Your mood became so dark and cold,
Every day was another test.
I begged for you to tell me what I had done wrong,
Where was the son I loved so much, where had that child gone?
You said you couldn't cope with the pressure, with the pain
Then you slammed the door that final time, as I cried out your name.
For months I didn't see you, I felt lost and so alone
Just waiting for that moment when you might call home.
Then the phone call came,
A friends of yours he said.
His voice was fraught and tearful and I could feel his distress.
So now I hold you once again, but your body is cold,
And the needle marks in your arms confirm what I've been told.
And as I stare into your eyes, and I see only death
You softly say 'I'm sorry Mum,' as you draw your final breath.

R Holmes

The Pit Heaps

Boyhood memories of a Durham village
couched in the shadow of a worked-out mine,
ringed by pit heaps like giant mole hills,
playground paradise - wet weather or fine.

Black hills alive with defiant grasses,
rose-purple willow herb and blackberry
swarming with bumble bees, spiders, red admirals,
exciting game for my brother and me.

Jam jar-swinging intrepid hunters
fearless of scratches, bites or stings,
eager to catch those prized 'red arsies',
shouts of triumph - sport of kings.

Some days we raced to the pit 'reservoy',
slippery-steep, broken-brick lined,
graveyard of junk - prams, bedsteads and bikes,
coal sacks with puppies and kittens still blind.

But the 'reservoy' newts were what we were after
especially the gloriously-crested males
with gleaming orange and black spotted bellies
darting away with a flash of their tails.

With home-made nets we caught then raced them
playing high stakes - proud possessions changed hands -
battle-scarred marbles, chewing gum, black bullets,
palm-smooth catapults with thick rubber bands.

Those halcyon summers seemed unending
as if the sun shone all the day
upon those everlasting pit heaps
that magnet-like drew us to play.

Ray Wilson

Smoke On The Moon

Far misting copse now close appears
In crisp at even snowfall new and
Playing foxes, rusted, bark aloud . . .
Where high and proud and five a side
Stark fish-bone treetops wave, astride
A long and climbing avenue.

Three trooping brothers trundle in,
Pack and cape, to glad escape from
Blood and more, to damn the war
With all its din . . . bedraggled . . .
Reach the Coaching Inn . . .
As winter's chancing sun reclines,
To disembark in lantern-shine.

A coachman speaks of too much snow,
The horses can no further go.
Thus armed with pay and full of mirth,
There, troopers drink to peace on earth.
Their battles won, they rest awhile but
On then! . . . Over brook and stile . . .
As would all brothers, three abreast,
Across such, push and shove in jest!

Snow on snow, deep they go, away the styx!
With boot print six, cruel the blow in
Field on field now 'dot' they three . . .
The 'domino' . . . black on white in this night
Seeking out the city bright.
No cannon-fire in drift and spire but
Late, down rutted freezing shire, come . . .
Echoes of cathedral choir.

Now folding snows shift well aside
For bustling streets all cobbled wide,
Where 'easy-women' shout out loud and
Lamplit 'work' a bawdy crowd.
With breath of heated kettle-steam,
Thus, stand the three within a dream,
They search out, frosted lash and eye,
A tavern, with no tankard dry . . . and
Not 'too soon' do they espy
A sign which swings a pretty tune . . .
All writ in gold 'Smoke On The Moon'.

Roger Mosedale

Soothing Surroundings

When the loudest thing
is a crow's flapping wing;
an endless spool of landscape
rolls across my vision.

When butterflies billow, forming soft frills,
with the rise and sweep of mist muffled hills;
every tiny sound of nature
echoes in my ear.

When bright poppies blaze in the morning sun
a blanket of lambs frolic in fun.
Sunbeams scatter diamonds
across the surface of the sea.

When bumble bees bask and drone
through summer air as still as stone;
a kaleidoscope of rainbows
play beneath my heavy lids.

When swallows skim, then glide unseen,
soft rain cries down on emerald green.
Soothed senses weave
and melt as one.

Rosalind Smith

The Handkerchief

It must have been her handkerchief
In crumpled crisis on the chair,
Whose crimson monograph, for grief,
lay bleeding in the shadows there.

And like a pennant having done
Some stirring and immortal deed,
Its gay profusion caught the sun,
And made the watching spirit bleed.

A symphony in lunar white,
I held its softness to my cheek,
And thought of some transfigured night
On love's divine and distant peak.

And music touched the inner ear
With songs of sweet regretfulness
To bring her incarnation near
From oceans of forgetfulness.

And smothered in familiar scents,
Oh, how my eyes dissolved in tears,
As when the contrite heart repents,
And sheds the burden of the years.

I thought of old, discarded joys,
And sweet misgivings, long since gone,
And youth and love in equipoise,
And dreams to hang their grief upon.

At last, I tossed the thing away,
As if it were my very heart,
And there, in white, my sorrows lay
Immortalised, as at the start.

S H Smith

The Visit

He is no stranger to this room
He enters quietly.
With stealthy touch he admires the bric-a-brac
Leaving his damp prints in the gloom.
She does not stir
She knows he is there
Feeling his breath upon her hair.
A shiver runs down her spine
Her hands clutch the blanket tighter.
He is her only visitor and gently folds
His arms around her.
She croons softly and dreams of blossomed fields
As her blood runs cold.
She stiffens
He is leaving
But no tears cloud her eyes.
They will never meet again.

People will know what happened here
In this lonely place
And will whisper the murderer's name
As they cover the old woman's face.

Death from natural causes . . . so the papers say.
But is it natural freezing to death.
Alone on Christmas Day . . .

S Nicolaou

Fingernails

Daddy always cut my nails too short.
As I bled and itched I'd know
He'd cause all future shortcomings.
Then . . .
Gone.
Swallowing with it masculine overtones
And the desire for independence.
Little would I know I had no nails
Left for revenge;
Or to grip.
They lie now, little crescents in the bath
To act as gravel in my shoe.
Temporary disappointments.

Sally Mavin

Bed And Breakfast

An aroma
Scents caressing a bed
Where stems of flowers have slept
. . . carved into bark . . .
leaves lie scattered
kisses of the forehead
hand touched face
arm touches face
face covers face
we lie flat
sleep takes an impatient
step backwards
as you gain strength
as I gain control over the situation
you lie back and gather thoughts of the day
reflecting

in the morning
perplexed and shy
we eat a toast to the new day
as marmalade kisses cover over coffee-stained
mouths

Sheila Coll

Anghofio (V. To Forget)

At the funeral of inspiration
I met Glyn again:
Not laughing in the quiet street
With familiar friends,
But limping politely
Through the soft, mourning drizzle.

He offered a *'Shwmae?'*
Before his tongue was bitten by English
And his Welsh, blown like
The rain around him, disappeared
With a weak, wet smile.

'I cannot speak the same as you, you see . . .'

He said shaking his head to the church path.
His feeble words were dressed
In a rich, rusting accent:
Like a tramp in an Armani suit.

'. . . you know prro-perr Welsh, you see!'

I offered my condolences
To his dear departed language,
And then thought about mine:
How long would it be until I
Stood at another silent graveside,
Without words fine enough
To express my grief?
With no Welsh between me and death.
Who would weep more
Weak, tired tears for me and
My forgotten song?
Who would hear two thousand
Years singing sadly,
Somewhere in the back of my skull
Like a maggot?

Stephen Mason

Leyna

The infinite matrix.

Contorted lonely rocks,
Cut and scoured by hollow waters,
Almost Lunar in their emptiness.

The cul-de-sacs of solitude,
Full of pot-holes,
Seeming easy,
Yet so tripping,
Grey
In their deception,

To be foiled by a young girl,
Floating freely through the mists,
Her infant's hands,
So fragile, steeped
In elegant simplicity.

Standing on the shore,
She asked for nothing in return,
Clearing paths
And tangled thoughts
Of years of fruitless work.

So I tried to make a world for her,
From soil, and plant, and air,
And together we built three bridges,
As the breeze blew through her hair.

When I turned to wave goodbye,
I found I couldn't let her go,
So I carried her across, so light,
She walks beside me now.
An old photograph,
Never taken, never seen,
Under the haunting cries of gulls,
Young Leyna of the sea.

Stuart R Boyd

First Time

He is not so sure-footed now
picking his way
down the sea-smoothed slate,
still wet and cold
beneath the hoof.

A brass-plate sun,
warms his rump
and the saddle,
sweats his back
as he noses the breeze.

Salt spray flares his nostrils
and he champs
the bit, foaming,
and feels the sand
yield to his hesitant stride.

Mounted, he is taken,
sugar-cubed
and whip-kissed,
towards the white
fizzing tide.

Further boy! Further still
the leather - lick urges,
but the backwash steals
his foothold
tugs his fetlocks.

Steady! Steady!
But he, wide-eyed
and snorting
rears roller-high
stamping the froth at his heels.

And again he faces the swell,
mastered , though not
pliant or willing until
heel-nudged, he turns
scenting home.

Sue Hansard

The Chase

Hear the master call them all to heel
Deep in the country on this lovely morn
Those Scarlet Riders trailing yapping hounds
Assemble for the meet, in answer to the horn

No eyes for the beauty that surrounds them
The woods, the paths, the flowers, pass ignored
As they congregate there ready for the chase
To hunt, to follow, all with one accord

Snorting horses impatient as their riders
Awaiting the signal for the 'sport' to start
And the knowing hounds expecting fun
From God's creatures, who will play a part

A blast from the horn and the rallying cry
Signals the start and away they all go
Follow the leader where he rides
Across the fields with the hounds before

A cry as the fox is first sighted
And the leader heads on to his trail
With the baying dogs picking his scent up
They surge on faster, they bark and they wail

Up and down the hills and dales
They track him, getting ever closer
Across the fields and over the brook
And the sniffing pack runs faster

Through the hedges and into the woods
They think they have him in a corner
But he gives them the slip and escapes
To run for a little while longer

He runs and runs for his life
He knows they are out to catch him
He slows half dead with lungs on fire
And there's no response from his limbs

So they set upon the fox lying there
Dead from drowning, in his own blood
From a ruptured heart and they tear
Him to pieces with fangs of blood

Terry Daley

The Unborn Child

Blue cotton slips through her ordered fingers.
Polished pine reflecting nimble garments
and their heavy-scented past.

Head gently bowed with clear eyes
sorrowed, observing the lilac flowers
and sweet refrains of those
who can no longer think.

A designated room
laid in preparation for their original chance
of a perfect creation.
Too many cards now clutter the space.

An ordinary Monday.
Rains falling into golden sunshine.
She is only left with the ashen remains
of her child left always to be.

Tina Coope

Over You

Considered I was over you,
Hadn't thought of you in weeks.

But then
You jammed the windscreen edge to edge
On sight,
And made me turn sharp left
Instead of going right.

Was certain you were ages past,
Hadn't thought of you in days.

But then
You filled the empty shelves of shops
It seems,
And made my heart inflate
Amongst the peas and beans.

Was sure I'd dumped you years ago,
Hadn't thought of you in hours.

But then
You stormed the café during lunch
You fool,
And made me seek your face
On every vacant stool.

Valerie Hockaday

For A Lost Sister

Half-formed, your sentences
Bleed into my sorrow
Here is no future
Here no tomorrow.

Once we slept
Cupped like teaspoons,
Shared childish dreams
Beneath the covers,
Whispered secrets like lovers.

Now your twilight world merges
Reality and illusion.
Cruel relentless days
Erase time's definition,
Erode your persona.

Longing for your return
I cling to memory's rags,
Yearn for recognition,
Grieve at this premature bereavement,
This death without a funeral.

Vera Morrill

Neglect

You held me in your prison
For far too many years
Restraining any freedom
Ignoring all my fears.
You trapped me in your darkness
Full of suspicion and decay
I loathed your every judgement
Yet endured it every day.

I flourished once, in adolescence
I grew to be so strong
Rising steadily like a rose
To be crushed by something wrong.
I cursed the heavens above me
As I thought they were to blame
For the hatred that grew inside me
Raging like a flame.

You disapproved of everything
And everyone who wasn't you
I despise everything you stood for
If only now you knew.
My desire is to defeat you
And win your wicked game
I'll fight for all my life is worth
I'll tolerate the pain.

No longer will I abide you
For the freedom now is mine
No longer will you rule me
For in this child you'll find
Love that you neglected
Life you overlooked
A person you disfigured
Another heart you took.

Vivienne Bern

The Sands Of Changi Beach

The Malayan dawn glowed like a warming ember,
Rekindled by eternal shame,
Changi jail towered above me,
Walls impregnated by their pain.

England's sons and fathers,
Like cattle, herded to the shore,
Tortured souls, shot and savaged,
The faceless, then no more.

The shifting sands of far off beaches
Shelter memories of their fight,
For survival. Retribution,
For their long forgotten plight.

The moving shores of Changi Beach, crawled with tiny crabs,
Harvesting the souls
Of the forgotten, of the long dead,
Far from beloved homes.

Now the white sands of the tide lines,
With their memories ebb and flow,
Carry rhythmically the pulses,
Of their heartbeats long ago.

Wendy Tetley

INFORMATION

We hope you have enjoyed reading this book - and that you will continue to enjoy it in the coming years.

If you would like to enter this year's competition, for more information contact:

Forward Press Top 100 Information
Remus House
Peterborough
PE2 9JX

Tel: 01733 898101
Fax: 01733 313524